D0908800

Science Matters
PULLEYS

James De Medeiros

WEIGL PUBLISHERS INC.

Published by Weigl Publishers Inc.
350 5th Avenue, Suite 3304, PMB 6G
New York, NY USA 10118-0069
Website: www.weigl.com

Library of Congress Cataloging-in-Publication Data

De Medeiros, James, 1975-
 Pulleys / James De Medeiros.
    p. cm. -- (Science matters)
 Includes index.
 ISBN 978-1-60596-041-8 (hard cover : alk. paper) -- ISBN 978-1-60596-042-5 (soft cover : alk. paper)
 1. Pulleys--Juvenile literature. I. Title.
 TJ1103.D45 2009
 621.8--dc22
                              2009001947

Printed in China
1 2 3 4 5 6 7 8 9 13 12 11 10 09

Editor Nick Winnick
Design and Layout Terry Paulhus

Photograph Credits

Weigl acknowledges Getty Images as its primary image supplier for this title.

All of the Internet URLs given in the book were valid at the time of publication. However, due to the dynamic nature of the Internet, some addresses may have changed, or sites may have ceased to exist since publication. While the author and publisher regret any inconvenience this may cause readers, no responsibility for any such changes can be accepted by either the author or the publisher.

Every reasonable effort has been made to trace ownership and to obtain permission to reprint copyright material. The publishers would be pleased to have any errors or omissions brought to their attention so that they may be corrected in subsequent printings.

Contents

What is a Pulley?

Pulleys can be found all around you. They are part of many machines, from cars to window shades. Pulleys, such as cranes, are often used in construction work to lift heavy objects.

A pulley is a wheel with a groove around the outside edge. In this groove, there is a rope or cable. Pulling on one side of the rope causes the wheel to turn. This moves the other end of the rope in the opposite direction.

■ Pulleys are one of six simple machines. People use simple machines to make daily tasks easier.

How do Pulleys Work?

Pulleys work by changing the direction of a force to make it easier to lift an object.

The simplest pulleys have one grooved wheel and a rope. The object, or **load**, to be lifted is attached to one end of the rope. Pulling down on the free end of the rope will lift the object up off the ground. This is because the wheel of the pulley changes the force from a downward pull to an upward lift.

This type of pulley is called a fixed pulley. The wheel stays fixed in place while the load and **effort** can move.

Push and Pull

Force is a push or a pull that moves an object or changes its direction. Gravity is the force that pulls objects toward Earth. The force of gravity gives objects weight. When an object is standing still, all of the forces pushing or pulling it are balanced. This balance is called **equilibrium**.

When scientists study how objects move, there are three facts that they need to know. They must know how much the object weighs and how fast it is moving. They must also measure the force that is causing the object to move.

■ During a game of tug of war, people pull with all their strength.

Forces in Action

Force is measured in Newtons. This measurement is named after Sir Isaac Newton. Newton was an English scientist who defined scientific laws of motion. These laws describe the ways that objects move and interact with each other.

A heavy object will exert many Newtons of force pushing downward. If you give your friend a push on a swing, the strength of that push can be measured in Newtons. The weight of a full two-liter soda pop bottle pushes down with a force of about 20 Newtons.

Uplifting Machines

Pulleys can provide a mechanical advantage. This means that they make work easier.

Imagine a heavy box attached to the rope of a pulley. The weight of the box is pushing down with 100 Newtons (N) of force. Using a fixed pulley, you would have to pull down on the rope with 100 N of force to move the box. This pulley system has no mechanical advantage. This is because both sides have the same amount of force pulling on them. To gain a mechanical advantage, the system must use a moveable pulley or more than one pulley.

● Fixed pulleys can be attached to helicopter frames to lift up objects.

Putting it All Together

A fixed pulley alone does not provide a mechanical advantage. To provide this, people can use moveable pulleys. Sometimes, they use many pulleys working together.

On a moveable pulley, the load is attached to the pulley itself. One end of the rope is tied in place. The user pulls the free end.

Using a fixed pulley and a moveable pulley together makes lifting a load easier. This is because each pulley supports half of the load. If the load weighs 100 N, each pulley supports 50 N. Pulling the rope with 50 N of force will lift the load. More pulleys can be added to the system to make lifting even easier.

Foiled by Friction

Friction is a force that is created when two objects rub against each other. In the case of pulleys, friction occurs between the rope and the wheel. The rougher the surfaces of the objects, the more friction is created.

Friction changes the force of motion into heat. This wastes some of the force that is needed to lift the load. It can also cause fast-moving pulleys to heat up or break.

■ Heat from friction can be reduced by adding oils or using smoother materials.

How is Friction Useful?

Friction is often harmful to simple machines. It can also be useful in some ways.

Many times, to move a load from place to place, it must be held in mid-air for long periods. To make holding loads in place easier, many pulleys have friction brakes.

Friction brakes help people using pulleys move loads slowly and easily. Friction brakes are flat pieces of metal or plastic that can clamp down on the rope or wheel of a pulley. Pressing tightly against the rope or wheel causes a high amount of friction. This friction keeps the pulley from moving.

Single Pulleys

A single pulley is the simplest kind of pulley. It can be either fixed or moveable. Single pulleys were used more often in the past, to move water or help build tall buildings.

Some simple devices still use single pulleys today, such as clotheslines or curtains. However, most modern pulleys are used as parts of more complex machines.

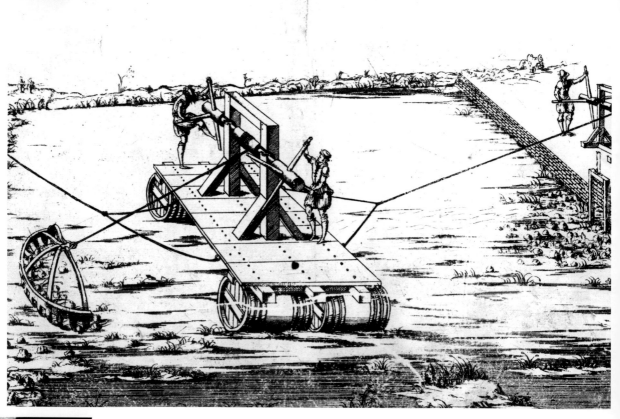

■ At one time, pulleys were used in machines that tilled soil.

Simple Strings

Clotheslines

In warm areas, people sometimes hang their clothes outside to dry. Wet clothes are clipped to a cord attached to a pulley at either end. Pulling on the cord causes it to move back and forth. Clothes can be pulled closer to the user, or pushed into the sunlight to dry.

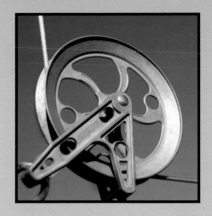

Flagpoles

Flagpoles have a simple pulley attached. The flag is attached to one side of the rope. Pulling on the other side raises the flag. Most official flags are raised in the morning and lowered at night.

Curtains

Curtains have simple string pulleys attached. Pulling on one of these strings will tug on the top edge of the curtain, pulling it open. Pulling the other side of the string will close the curtains.

Pulling Together

Today, machines that use pulleys often include more than one of them. Pulleys are combined together to give people more control over how an object is lifted. They also make loads even easier to lift. These systems are called compound pulleys. They are often attached to motors and are sometimes completely **automatic**.

■ Combining multiple pulleys can greatly increase the mechanical advantage they give.

Roped In

Modern pulleys work together with other simple machines to create complex machines.

Drive Belt

Car engines use a special type of pulley called a drive belt. A belt is a band of rubber wrapped tightly around several pulley wheels. When one wheel turns, the belt turns as well. This transfers the power from that wheel to the others connected to the belt.

Winches

Winches are used in many construction sites and machine shops. They can be attached to cranes or to the ceiling of a building. Winches use many pulleys at once in order to lift very heavy objects. Winches lift everything from motors to steel beams.

History on the Ropes

Pulleys have been used for thousands of years. Some stories from ancient Mesopotamia mention pulleys being used to lift jars of water as early as 1500 BC. Pulleys also have been used in the construction of many tall structures throughout history. These include the Colosseum in Rome, Italy, and the Cathedral of Notre Dame in Paris, France.

Pulleys were very important on sailing ships. Ships moved by catching the wind in their sails. Pulleys were used to raise and lower the sails of a ship. This would change the amount of wind hitting the sail. Sailors used this to change their speed and direction. Motor boats are more common today, but many ships still use sails.

■ People with solid footing on the ground could use pulleys to raise heavy stones or timbers to workers high above.

The Power of One

More than 2,000 years ago, a scientist named Archimedes discovered a great deal about how simple machines work. He found that, if he used pulleys properly, he could lift nearly any object.

Archimedes wrote to a Greek king named Hieron with news of his discoveries. The king had a large ship that he knew would be difficult to move. He asked Archimedes to move it.

Before allowing Archimedes to try moving the ship, Hieron loaded it with heavy objects. Archimedes set to work making a system of many pulleys. All of the pulleys working together had a great mechanical advantage.

Archimedes was able to lift and move the ship as easily as if it were sailing on the ocean.

Gaining an Advantage

There are six simple machines. They are *inclined planes*, *levers*, *pulleys*, *screws*, *wedges*, and the *wheel and axle*. All simple machines are designed to make work easier. These machines do not have batteries or motors. They do not add any **energy** of their own to help people do work. So, how do simple machines work?

Simple machines work by changing the forces that are applied to them. In most cases, they do this by changing the distance or direction of a force.

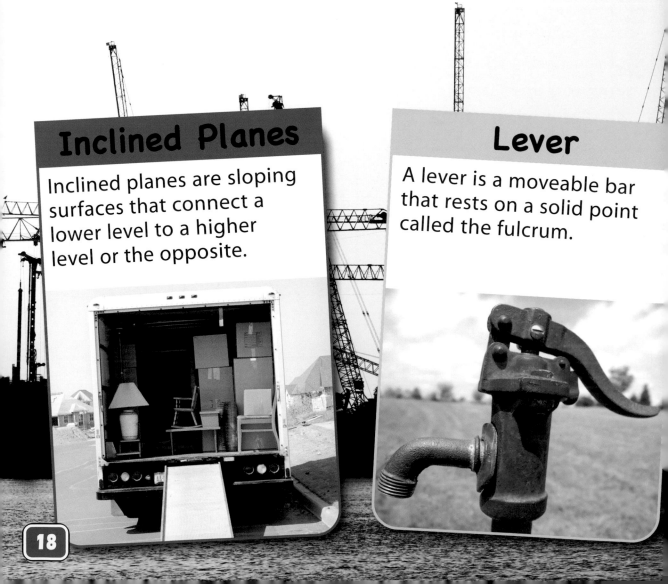

Inclined Planes

Inclined planes are sloping surfaces that connect a lower level to a higher level or the opposite.

Lever

A lever is a moveable bar that rests on a solid point called the fulcrum.

Pulley

pulley is a wheel with a roove around the outside dge. In this groove, there a rope or cable. Pulling he rope turns the wheel.

Screw

Screws are tube-shaped tools with sharp edges spiralling around them. They are often used to fasten objects together.

Wedge

A wedge is a triangle-shaped tool with a sharp edge. It can separate two objects, lift an object, or hold an object in place.

Wheel and Axle

Wheels are circle-shaped objects that rotate around their center. They often have an axle in the middle to hold them in place.

Surfing Simple Machines

How can I find more information about pulleys and other simple machines?
- Libraries have many interesting books about simple machines.
- Science centers can help you learn more about force, motion, and friction through hands-on experiments.
- The Internet offers some great websites dedicated to simple machines.

Where can I find a good reference website to learn more about pulleys?
Encarta Homepage
www.encarta.com
- Type any term related to simple machines into the search engine.
  Some terms to try include "pulley" and "mechanical advantage."

Science in Action

Make Your Own Pulley

Try making a pulley to help you lift objects more easily. To complete the experiment, you will need:

- a door and the doorknob handle
- a bottle of water
- a long string

1. Tie one end of the string to the spout of the water bottle.
2. Place the string in the groove, or middle part, of the doorknob between the doorknob and the door. Make sure that the bottle is on one side of the grooved area of the doorknob. The other side of the string should be on the opposite side of the doorknob.
3. Pull the free end of the string downward. The more you pull the string down, the higher the bottle will move. Is there any friction slowing down the string as you pull it?

What Have You Learned?

1 What is a pulley?

2 While using a pulley, when is friction caused?

3 On a pulley, where does the rope, chain, belt, or cable pass?

4 When all of the forces on an object are balanced, what is that balance called?

5 What kind of pulley only has the load attached to the pulley itself?

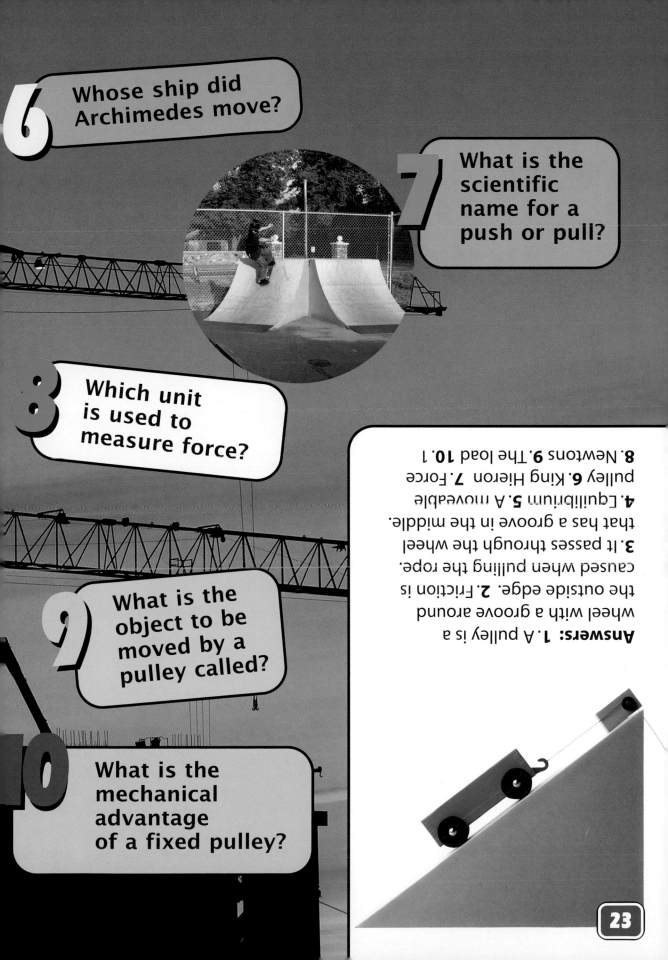

6 Whose ship did Archimedes move?

7 What is the scientific name for a push or pull?

8 Which unit is used to measure force?

9 What is the object to be moved by a pulley called?

10 What is the mechanical advantage of a fixed pulley?

Answers: 1. A pulley is a wheel with a groove around the outside edge. **2.** Friction is caused when pulling the rope. **3.** It passes through the wheel that has a groove in the middle. **4.** Equilibrium **5.** A moveable pulley **6.** King Hieron **7.** Force **8.** Newtons **9.** The load **10.** 1

Words to Know

automatic: works by itself, without human control

effort: the amount of work it takes to move an object

energy: power needed to do work

equilibrium: a state when all the forces acting on an object are balanced

force: the pushing or pulling on an object

load: the object or substance being worked on by a simple machine

Index

DATE			

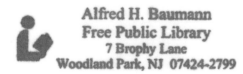